TEACH MY CAT TO DO THAT

TEACH MY CAT TO DO THAT

Simple tricks for your four-legged friend

**Jo-Rosie Haffenden
and Nando Brown**

BOXTREE

First published 2017 by Boxtree
an imprint of Pan Macmillan
20 New Wharf Road, London N1 9RR
Associated companies throughout the world
www.panmacmillan.com

ISBN 978-0-7522-6642-8

1 3 5 7 9 8 6 4 2

A CIP catalogue record for this book is available from the British Library.

Typeset by seagulls.net
Printed and bound by CPI Group (UK) Ltd, Croydon, CR0 4YY

Visit **www.panmacmillan.com** to read more about all our books
and to buy them. You will also find features, author interviews and
news of any author events, and you can sign up for e-newsletters
so that you're always first to hear about our new releases.

Contents

Foreword
by Alexander Armstrong

I never quite know what answer to give when I'm asked if I'm a 'cat' or 'dog' person, because the truth is I'm very much both. I've lived with cats *and* dogs for as long as I can remember but I expect very different behaviours from each. If I went for a long walk and the cat was tailing me all the way, I think I'd find it a bit unsettling. Equally if every time I read the paper on the kitchen table the dog kept walking up and down the page, trying to rub itself against my face, I suspect I'd see that in a less-than-endearing light. We condition our expectations of animal behaviour according to what we know but – as this excellent book demonstrates – perhaps we are underestimating our pets by setting the bar so low. Animals, as we have known for centuries, are capable of acquiring truly breathtaking skills. This may be sheepdogs performing feats of herding to simple verbal commands or the fabulous Pudsey wowing us, and the *BGT* judges, with his dexterity. But it wasn't until I'd seen Jo-Rosie and Nando train a chicken to perform a challenging piece of choreography and a rook to tidy up a room and put all the mess into a basket that I realized quite how much can be achieved. There is a whole world of fun to be had with our pets; a world we can access through simple training techniques that we, and they, can pick up in no time.

The story always goes that dogs are easy to train because they're … well, what's the word … biddable? Whereas cats

are just way too clever to do what we want – too cool for school. Garfield was always far more aware of what was really going on than the bouncy, excitable Odie, but then I suspect Garfield's creator, Jim Davis, was avowedly a 'cat' person, don't you? And you only have to think about all those guide dogs, sniffer dogs and therapy dogs to realize that you can't write off the whole species as 'easily bought'. But far more importantly, we need to recognize that cats CAN be trained. Cats build up all kinds of behaviours – just think of how many daily routines your own cats might have. Over the years I've probably owned (ha! If a cat could hear me say that) twelve cats or more and they all perfected or had interesting and unique little tricks. One of ours used to say 'thank you' when you opened a door or window for him – he'd mewl and howl to be let in and, when you finally relented, he'd parp out a little mini-purr as he hopped past. (I assume it was 'thank you'; it may have been something unrepeatable.) But the key is that cats love affection and they love treats (even Garfield would back me up here), so there's a very direct way to reward certain behaviours and build up a system for learning.

The connection you make with an animal through training is something awe-inspiring and truly special. Instead of merely enjoying the company of the animal you love, you are taking your relationship to a completely new level and forging a deep bond of understanding that turns owning a pet into a two-way partnership that brings huge pleasure and fulfillment to both of you. All the more so if it's with a supposedly 'aloof' cat. So set yourself small but achievable goals and you'll be amazed at how quickly you progress. And remember at all times: if a chicken can dance, a cat can do ANYTHING. Have fun and good luck!

Introduction

For most people, the words 'teach' and 'cat' do not belong in
the same sentence. Whenever we travel the world, meeting
pets and their owners, we seem to hear the same descriptions
when people talk about cats: aloof, arrogant and disdainful.
While their loyal and friendly dogs are their absolute best
friends, cats are more like a hostile housemate, grudgingly
accepting their company. And the internet confirms
these suggestions. A quick search online for 'dog tricks'
immediately yields stars like *Ziggy Tricks* or *Jumpy*, famous
for their obedience and their impressive tricks, while on the
flip side we have *Grumpy Cat* – famous for simply having
a grumpy face. Most people's attitude towards teaching
felines can be summed up by the video of a cat disdainfully
knocking a glass off the table and watching it smash.

Now, while it's true that cats certainly are different to
dogs, and especially when it comes to being trained, they
are actually capable of learning just as well as dogs. The
approaches you need to take towards developing a training
routine should be tailored to them, and they are not trained
in exactly the same way, but it's perfectly possible to teach a
cat new tricks if you make sure you are aware that it's a cat
you are training – not a dog! And it isn't just that you *can*
train cats; cats actually love being trained.

What we've heard, time and time again, is that the
process of trick training reveals a whole new side to people's
cats: a new relationship upon which trust, love and mutual
respect are the underpinnings. The first stage of training is

to learn what your cat likes and is happy doing, and what they need from their environment. As a result of these key foundations, you'll find training is an amazing way to get to know your cat. Secondly, you'll see how the changes in your relationship as a result of trick training will improve the wellbeing of your cat.

They might not be bounding off after a stick, tongue lolling out, any time soon, but the focused attention you pay to your cat as part of this learning process is a wonderful way of deepening and enriching your relationship with them. And, if you put in the training hours, then who knows, they might just surprise you!

Because, let's face it, even though they may be moody, wilful and downright aloof sometimes, we love them anyway.

Jo-Rosie and Nando

The Truth About Cats and Dogs

When and why did cats obtain this reputation for wilful disobedience when dogs got all the credit for brains and earned the title of man's best friend? Where does this myth come from?

Well, the domestication of animals began when we humans started living in settlements. Dogs learnt there were huge benefits to be had from staying close to us. We put out our rubbish, and this was suddenly a great food source. Cats, however, went about things a bit differently …

We started growing crops to eat and, with this cultivation of the land and growing of nice edible plants, so came an influx of small furry animals. And, as any *Tom and Jerry* fan will tell you, where there are mice, our feline friends follow in hot pursuit. This difference in the history of their domestication laid the foundation for the difference in character between cats and dogs. Unlike dogs, who saw humans as a new source of nourishment, cats smartly avoided direct contact and merely hung about in the fields close to where people lived. It made evolutionary sense to be around crops and fields, but avoiding people themselves was also beneficial to cats.

While dogs discovered that sticking close to people meant the best access to the best food, cats learnt that keeping their distance and knowing the lie of the land would ultimately ensure a thriving population. To ensure they thrived, cats would pick an area and mark their scent all around it using scent glands on their neck, the pads of their paws and at the sides of their mouths. This scent marked out an area that became their territory. Cats don't hunt together, so they guard their own space for hunting as if their lives depended on it – because they once did!

Independence is thus natural for cats, as is their desire to make mental maps about the area in which they live. Cats are very particular creatures and, while many dogs are pretty easygoing, our cats live by very specific rules. They don't like change, unfamiliar scenarios or places that could suggest danger. It's key to keep that in mind when you are beginning training.

Top 5 Rules to Keep Your Cat Happy at Home

Top 5 Rules to Keep Your Cat Happy at Home

1. I need lots of food little and often.

Cats are stealthy hunters but many of their hunting expeditions leave them empty pawed. With that in mind, knowing where likely sources of food are located becomes very important. Little and often is the way to the cat's stomach and, in nature, they may eat between twelve to twenty mini-meals a day. They are actually, scientifically speaking, more proficient problem solvers than dogs, and cats that remembered where the good stuff came from thrived. Not just that but, unlike dogs, they can exhibit excellent self-control when it comes to food. Did you know that the best way to feed a cat is to constantly keep out a fresh supply of food? Yep – while a dog may eat himself to obesity, cats have proven themselves to be fantastic self-regulators, eating only what their bodies require.

2. My water must be clean and fresh and apart from my food source.

Clean, fresh water is so important to the cat. With various genetic and physiology issues – which result in a high propensity for kidney and liver problems as well as a susceptibility to urinary tract infections and cystitis – not having access to fresh water can literally kill a cat. Unsurprisingly this biological need can make cats extremely aware of their water supply and actually, unbeknown to many cat owners – and with fresh water being key to survival – having food and drink in the same place next to each other can cause extreme stress to cats.

3. You must not mess with my system or move stuff around.

Many cat owners laugh at the fact that a simple furniture change seems to cause their cat a nervous breakdown. Well, the ability to know their territory like the back of their paw is what has enabled cats to thrive. Cats hunt on their own, and will mark out territory using scent glands on their necks and their claws. That's right, folks, they don't just scratch the sofa to sharpen their claws or to infuriate you, they are actually marking out their territory to ensure it's theirs to hunt in. This important need for cats to know their environment – which territory leaves them vulnerable and where the best hunting spots are – makes it a little easier to understand why they hate change so much.

4. Don't change what you do, ever. In fact, don't change anything.

And that goes for routines, too. Patterns in their behaviour mark when they will be fed and where water and play will come from. Routine is what helps them make sense of living in our human world. While cats cannot tell the time as we do, they are nevertheless aware of time. We know this because a cat will know when to return to prey and when the animal they've killed will have become rotten. They are also aware of breakfast and dinner when they live in a domestic home, so when their owners go MIA, or when a new baby disrupts the waiting resident cat's opportunity to feed, a cat may even vacate the premises and choose to live somewhere new!

5. I will like you better if you play hunting games with me.

Cats need to hunt. They have a sequence of behaviours that includes targeting their prey with their eyes, ears and that very clever nose, stalking stealthily towards it, getting as close as possible without it realizing, then – when the prey moves and realizes they are being hunted by a cat – chasing the prey as fast as they can, eventually grabbing it with their teeth, killing the prey, possessing it and moving it to a safe place, then dissecting and consuming it.

As a result of this hunting sequence of behaviours being biologically reinforcing (they need to perform these behaviours and performing them means their species will thrive), the body also makes doing it feel good. When cats live in a home setting, an urban environment with a high cat population or as house cats, they don't often get an opportunity to practise the 'target, stalk, chase, grab-bite, kill-bite, possess and parade, dissect, consume' routine. Compassionate cat owners will give them opportunities to

practise these movements with special rod toys, which are like fishing rods but instead of a hook on the line there is usually a fluffy toy. Playing with your cat will really increase their attachment bond with you.

If you play, remember the order of the sequence and try to move your toy to pantomime each part. Make your toy slow and pottering around when the cat is eying it up; hold it still for the cat to stalk, then, at the last moment, make the toy dart out in front of your cat for her to chase. Then, when your cat first grabs the toy, give a little fight and eventually let your cat 'kill' the toy and encourage the parade. Cats are SO much fun to play with and, if they could speak, they would definitely thank you for it!

Selecting Your Cat: Finding the Purrfect Pupil

While cats have a smaller brain than dogs, they do prove that size isn't everything. They have more neurons firing in the part of the brain used during problem solving. Not only that, but in some studies cats will outperform dogs on basic problem solving and 'find the food' tests. So what's going on? Why is it that we only ever see dogs performing on *Britain's Got Talent*?

Well, as we have described already, the cat domestication process has enabled our feline friends to keep their title of 'the wild ones'. But even though they have the capability to perform cool tricks, the issue of **owner focus** (the desire to concentrate on what their owner is doing), plus the wariness of performing in new and different settings, often means they won't perform. Simply put, cats don't like new things, or situations that put them in danger, or change. However, that doesn't mean that you can't create an environment within your home that means a cat feels able to do tricks as impressive as anything you'd see a dog do.

If you do want your cat to be one confident kitty when it comes to doing tricks out and about, selecting the right kitten or cat and then desensitizing him or her is your best bet.

Not all cats are made for the spotlight
Just like us, each cat is an individual – they are a rough mix of biology, environment and learning. Some are shy, some

are bold and many sit somewhere in the middle. As a result of this, just like us, some cats love training and want to perform acts of trickery to delight and amuse; others less so. Over the coming pages we'll give you the tools to see what sort of attitude your cat might have towards training, as well as the techniques you can use with any cat. However, it's worth bearing in mind that some breeds are more suited to training than others.

In regards to the biological ingredient, remember that when we breed an animal for a specific look, we are manipulating certain genes. Groups of genes linked to particular physical characteristics (let's say folded ears, like the Scottish Fold, or a short bobtail, like the Manx) can also lead to certain behaviour trends. With that in mind, choosing a breed of cat that is more likely to be outgoing, human-centric and curious will certainly make life easier for trick training. Highbred cats like the Savannah, the Toyger and, our favourite to train, the Bengal, are all these things and tend to be exceptionally easy to motivate as well. That said, as is often the case, the beauty and the brains come with a pay-off. While these breeds are favoured for training, they also come with a hefty price tag and are extremely high maintenance to live with! They require a lot more mental stimulation, as well as careful and safe physical exercise. In addition to this, many owners choose to keep these highly intelligent animals inside as house cats, due to the fear of them being stolen or run over. These are valid fears for these breeds, but ensuring the cat has enough access to what he or she needs is then often as time-consuming as having a dog.

Other breeds that are brilliant to train, like the Siamese and the Tonkinese, fit into this category but are probably only for owners who don't mind bearing the responsibilities of an extremely noisy, demanding young-child equivalent.

What all these breeds have going for them in the trainability department they lack in the 'easy to live with' ratings. That goes for the Sphinx, too. While extremely striking, with about as much hair as Nando, these cats drive home the message that the more trainable the cat, the less easy they tend to be to live with.

Although beautiful, cats and kittens from feral backgrounds, as well as breeds with a shorter history of domestication, like the Rex, do not tend to make good training companions. With the genetic background of each cat creating a window of possibilities regarding how tame or untamed a cat is likely to be, even the best-laid socialization plans have fallen flat with kittens who come from more feral backgrounds. Whilst working at the animal hospital, we saw full litters of feral kittens that had to be hand reared and still ended up frightened and completely overwhelmed by the prospect of being in a domestic pet home.

With all that in mind, you can't beat a well-socialized moggy for a good balance. A carefully chosen, confident 'Heinz 57' cat with nice friendly parents can go a long way in the training stakes, but will also not create chaos and havoc in the home like the highbred.

When looking at kittens for training, rescue centres are a great place to start. Kittens that have been hand reared, due to losing their parents or being rejected, can make great training cats. Natural human focus goes a long, long way, and these little guys have had to be very human focused during a formative period of their lives.

If you are selecting a kitten to train from a litter, ensure you get to meet both parents. While cats can be a little wary with strangers at the best of times, your kitty's parents should be outgoing, confident and curious. If you enter their space, you would hope to see them sniffing around your things and approaching you for affection, or even just investigating to see what you're all about. They should be excited around your breeder and eager to solicit attention and affection – look for shoulder rubs against legs, meowing at the owner and a generally high disposition. If you are looking for a cat to train we would recommend against cats with parents who are low in posture, hiss, have pinned ears or a tail that looks like a rattlesnake. Additionally, purring is one of those things, like a dog's waggy tail, which doesn't always mean a cat is happy. Cats also purr when they are very stressed, so make sure, if you do choose your kitten from a breeder, that you really look at the posture and personality of the parents.

The kitten you choose should be a bright spark. Ask the breeder which one escaped out of the box fastest, which was quickest to wean, which kitten plays the most – these are the kinds of things you're looking for. A kitten that, at an early age, seems cocky and fun loving is going to be the best kitten to train. While a more balanced and loving kitten would make a great pet, the little monkey with a nose for food and a taste for trouble might just be that feline Einstein you're looking for!

The same is true if you are getting a rescue cat from a shelter. Arguably you are better off picking a rescue cat for a trick cat – for reasons besides ethics. With a rescue cat you are making a selection from cats that are already formed characters. They have usually come through adversity and managed life in a rescue centre. If they continue to be optimistic and food motivated, as well as handler focused and bold, then you are onto a winner.

But how do you test if your cat is the right cat for the job?

Testing Your Cats: Trainability Tests

There are no tests your cat can take to tell you how intelligent it is. When you look at intelligence, it really is species specific. The only true test of intelligence for a cat would be to measure how much territory she has secured, how many babies she has produced, how much food they have managed to procure and how good they are at hunting over their lifetime, and then compare that to other cats who lived to the same age in the same kind of area.

What we are really looking at in this chapter is how to test the trainability of your cat.

There are four key attributes that the most trainable cats have:

- **Handler Focus** – wanting to work with their human partner, as a team.
- **Optimism** – the right cat will always assume it can win. This helps with a 'keep going' attitude, which ensures they will enjoy the little puzzles that trick training will present.
- **A Bold Attitude** – this is about more than just confidence; it's about curiosity and a desire to explore new opportunities.
- **Food Motivation** – a drive to work for food is going to make training faster and simpler for our feline friends.

While it is not imperative to find all four qualities in your new training buddy, if your cat does score high across the board, you know you're onto a winner. For cats that don't do well in any test, well, perhaps taking photos of your cat snubbing you will earn you quicker internet notoriety! Most cats will score high in some of these tests and lower in others; these cats are most definitely trainable, but check out the exercises that may help your cat to improve on those attributes where he presents lowest.

Handler Focus

1. Get a plastic bowl.
2. Tempt your cat with some lovely food (recommendation for this would be something like tuna, which has a pungent smell and is very palatable).
3. Place the food under the bowl.
4. As soon as your cat gets to the bowl, lift it like a half-open lid, so the food is exposed to him to get to, but you are kept there holding it. Allow him to finish.
5. Place a second piece of food down. This time, place your food under the bowl.
6. Count aloud how long it takes for your cat to ask you for help. Asking for help could be: 1) looking at you three times in a row or for a count of three; 2) meowing, because actually the cat has developed this vocalization since coming to live with us and it is thought that the meow is used by cats specifically to get our attention, or 3) clawing at your leg and not the bowl.

Scoring

1–3 seconds: his world revolves around you. (3)

3–10 seconds: you're definitely friends. (2)

10 seconds +: humans are there to giveth food, not taketh away. (1)

For cats that struggle with handler focus

Go and buy a rod toy. These are the ultimate in cat fun and games. Play as though the fluffy little toy on the end is alive and running away from your cat. Playing hunting games with you will cause your cat to release not only dopamine (which will get him excited and wanting to play again) but also oxytocin, which will help you both bond. Not a hunter? You could try hand feeding your cat to help increase their desire to be around you.

Optimistic Or Pessimistic

1. Get two bowls.

2. Get some super-yummy and smelly food that your cat loves (again, some kind of fish will work well for this).
3. Slice your fish into four portions.
4. Keep your cat shut out and place food in one of the bowls then place that bowl on the left-hand side of the room.

5. Place the empty bowl on the right-hand side of the room, closer to your cat's entrance than the second full bowl.
6. Allow your cat in to eat the food.
7. After he has finished the left bowl, see if he still goes and checks the right-hand bowl.
8. Repeat this test over four days and count how many times your cat goes to the right-hand bowl despite there never being food in it.

Scoring

4/4 days of checking the other bowl at some point or attempts at finding food in the empty bowl: your cat is a true optimist and will stop at nothing to prove that the world is wonderful. (3)

2–3/4 attempts at finding food in the empty bowl: realistic with her expectations, your cat will give things a shot but won't risk looking like a greedy Labrador for the sake of a few fish bits. (2)

0–1/4 attempts at finding food in the empty bowl: the humans are not to be trusted. Too often they open tins and then deny me! (1)

For cats who have a pessimistic outlook

Your cat needs to learn that sometimes they are lucky too. To help your cat become more optimistic, divide their daily portion of food in half. Feed them half as you usually would, straight from a dish, and hand out the other half as little bonuses throughout the day. For instance, call her in from outside and hand her a bit of food in her dish; after a nice stroke, get her a little snack; hide some inside the cat flap as a nice surprise when she returns from an unsuccessful hunt. She will soon become all purrs!

Bold Or Shy

This test can be really hard – if you already know your cat is shy you can skip this one and refrain from putting him through the stress of moving furniture and scary sounds.

1. Open the pots and pans cupboard in your kitchen.
2. Take out half the pots and pans and stack them around the entrance to the cupboard.
3. Get a handful of cat kibble or some yummy sliced cocktail sausage and place the treats around the pots and pans and inside the cupboard. Place a few bits in the pots and pans too.
4. Call your cat in and allow them to explore.

Scoring

Took all the treats, including from inside the pot: Columbus
   the cat. (3)

*Took the treats from around and inside the cupboard but not
   from inside the pot:* Dora the explorer. (2)

*Took the treats from around the pots but didn't dare venture
   into the pot or the cupboard:* Scaredy cat. (1)

For cats who are super shy

Retest your cat on the pots and pans every day. Add other
little adventures where she has to explore new things and
textures to find food. Splitting up her morning and evening
portion and hiding it around the house for her to find will
also encourage her to be a bit more curious.

Motivated By Food

1. Take ten treats.
2. Feed one to your cat for nothing.
3. Count to two and, if your cat is still hanging around for another treat, feed him another.

4. Repeat this process but make him wait double the time between each treat.
5. On the last treat your cat will be waiting almost twenty minutes for that little bit of food!

Scoring

Didn't give up before treat 8: Labracat. (3)

Stuck around until treat 5–7: Up for it. (2)

Gave up before treat 5: Desperate to fit into that catkini this summer. (1)

For cats that aren't particularly food orientated

Try lots of different treats to see if your cat will work for certain foods but not others. Natural Instinct make some amazing raw cat treats when the less expensive but highly popular high-street treats just don't cut the mustard. Also try human foods such as bacon and sausage. If your cat is still turning up her nose you could try playing with toys instead, although this will make the training process longer.

Overall scoring

9 points or more: you'll dash through this faster than Tom chasing Jerry.

5–8 points: if you work on the attributes where your cat didn't score very highly, you could most definitely get some cool tricks under your belt.

0–5 points: not naturally trainable, your cat is still super smart but you might be better off working on the more basic exercises.

Training

Training

Setting Up the Environment for Cat Training

Cats are all about territory. Do you remember we spoke about the Top 5 cat rules, and we described how cats are very picky about their mind maps and hate it when things change? Well, because of that they are not usually very confident in new environments. For *Teach My Pet to Do That*, series one, we actually couldn't find any cats to come to Pet School. Whilst a lot of people who auditioned had great cats with brilliant starter skills, none of them could cope in a brand-new environment. Hopefully in the future we will have more cats at the school, but they will have to have been sufficiently socialized. The great thing is that the techniques we use on the show will work perfectly with cats at home.

Jo used to have a Bengal called Millie. As she followed the 'selecting a purrfect pupil' steps above, Millie was already genetically predisposed to be bold and outgoing and also had a super-confident nature. However, Jo also worked hard to enhance this natural capacity. When Millie was a kitten, Jo used to take her food shopping in the supermarket in her pocket. Millie rode the bus. Millie visited a school and a farm and regularly rode the commuter train. After training, Millie was able to do many adverts and star in plenty of fashion photoshoots, including for *Vogue*! This was only possible due to careful socialization.

When socializing a cat it is really important that we enhance their natural resilience. To do this we have to inoculate them against new things and places and counter-condition them. That means they need slow and gradual exposure for short amounts of time, frequently – and then they need nice things (like special food and play) to happen in these nice places. When cats are taken into new situations but are unable to escape and are held captive, this isn't socialization – this is called 'flooding'. Sadly, many cat socializers do this unknowingly, unable to read the signs. When cats experience flooding they eventually give up trying to escape and, instead, shut down. This is called 'learnt helplessness'. When cats enter this state there is no way you will train them. It is very unpleasant for the cat and can actually cause damage to their brain. When the body suffers allostatic load – which is when a cat shows you he or she is stressed by licking their lips, yawning, muscle tension, fixed glaze, stress purring and body tension – but they can't escape (they are in a cat box or being held and unable to hide), they suffer damage to parts of the brain including the hippocampus. This means that in the future the cat will find it harder to show they are stressed, experience more stress in more situations, and can suffer with problems remembering things. Avoid this by being super-aware of your cat's happiness. Happy cats are generally curious and move slowly to sniff and explore their environment – but they are still happy to return to you and engage for a favourite treat.

Spot the signs

If you want to socialize your cat so they can do training in public, you'll need to be able to spot the signs of cat stress and avoid pushing your cat into stressful situations. Instead,

ensure they have frequent little exposures to the things you want them to get used to (like going to new places, training in different people's houses, or in children's parks where there are no dogs, or going on a lead and harness) and pair these experiences with food.

Preparing Your Training Area

Setting up a cat-training environment is pretty easy. All you need is a surface to train on and another surface to keep your stuff on. Don't attempt to keep your stuff on your training surface or you'll spend the entire session getting frustrated that your cat keeps helping himself to the snacks!

Preparation is everything, so follow the **What You Will Need** part of each training session prior to bringing the cat into the space.

Allow enough time and a few initial sessions for the cat to spend five minutes in the newly organized space getting treats for free. That way he will feel optimistic and confident about returning and hanging out in that space when it's time to train. Equally this will give him an opportunity to explore and check everything out so that he feels safe.

Remember when you train to keep distractions away to begin with. So if you live with multiple pets, curious kids, or if you have recently started a knitting project that is taking over the room, don't train until you can have your training space as clear as possible. While we want the cat to be able to perform tasks in real life, we want to provide the ultimate easy space to learn in first. If I put you in a nice, clear and clean space to learn maths equations it would be tricky; now if I tried to teach you maths equations on the commuter train from Brighton to London amid a host of your friends getting on and off, it would be nearly impossible.

There is an order to the learning in this book, which we very much recommend you follow.

Firstly, it involves breaking each exercise into lots of small sessions and doing them in your training area. Cats are notoriously stressed outside of their territory and animals struggle to learn new things under stress. In the first instance, train your cat to perform a trick reliably when asked in her training area, where he feels comfortable, and then start branching out.

Once a trick is reliable (meaning you would be happy to bet us £50 that your cat could do it five times in a row in the training area) you simply take your cat to other parts of their territory to practise. There will be lots of other distractions in different areas, and this will solidify the animal's knowledge of the trick. Once totally reliable in all the different areas of your cat's territory, you can start taking him to the places where you have socialized him and practise there too.

We would hold off giving any of the tricks a name until the cat is doing the whole trick. So that means we don't ask her to sit until your cat will happily sit for a treat. And until your cat learns the whole sequence of retrieving his collar (pick up, walk with it in his mouth, touch your hand, let go) before you ask your cat to 'bring me your collar'. This is so the cat doesn't learn that 'bring me the collar' just means 'pick up the collar'. It makes more sense to the animals we train to bring in cues – words that tell the animal they will be paid for performing the desired action – only once they understand the FULL action required.

The
Fundamentals

To train any animal, there are two essential elements: 1) they must understand what you want them to do and know when they've done it, and 2) they must want to do it through associating it with rewards.

Throughout this book we will use the terms 'mark' and 'reward' or 'mark' and 'reinforce' your cat to describe when we want you to pinpoint (mark) that your cat has done it, and when we want you to pay your cat for doing it (reward/reinforce).

Marking

We will often talk about marking behaviours. As at Pet School, we suggest using a marker when you are training your cat. Marker training is a fabulous way to help cats understand what we  require from them. A marker can be any distinct noise. That means it might be, as we used with River, a clicker; or it might be a particular word like 'yes', 'good' or 'ace'; it could be a flash of a torch if your cat is deaf, or a whistle if they are blind. All that matters is that it is consistent and that the behaviour the cat is performing when the marker happens

means 'THAT is what is earning you this treat'. Once a cat understands that the mark is given at the same time they perform the behaviour that gets them the reward, they will learn to repeat what has been marked. From there, training is much clearer.

For example: when we are teaching my cat to beg we will use a treat to first get her into a sit, then lure her front legs up. When we first practise, we can mark as soon as her legs leave the surface. If she is experienced with marker training she will then

understand that in order to receive more rewards she will need to repeat this behaviour.

This concept of using a marker to explain to the animal precisely what they need to repeat has been popular since marine trainers brought it to the dog-training world in the early 1980s. Strangely, it isn't popular with cat owners, who tend to believe their feline friends are beyond help!

Reinforcement

Operant conditioning has been used to train animals since 1905, when a man called Edward Thorndike did an experiment with cats, among other species, in boxes. He basically founded the notion that you can increase behaviour by adding something – which is positive reinforcement; you can increase behaviour by taking something away – which is called negative reinforcement; you can reduce behaviour by adding something – which is called positive punishment; and you can reduce behaviour by taking something away – which is negative punishment. While these days we understand that a lot of punishment-based techniques aren't very useful, as they cause stress to the animal, which can ruin a relationship, in those days we understood less about cats' emotions.

With our modern-day cat training we always want to increase behaviour, so we are always looking for reinforcement. Positive reinforcement includes food and toys and strokes and tickles; negative reinforcement includes removing something the animal needs to attain their treat – for example, removing the target they need to touch to get the treat when they get it wrong. Generally cats learn best with positive reinforcement. Notice that when we talk about reinforcement we specifically ask that you use rewards but don't suggest what those rewards are. That's because, even though we have made it clear that having a cat that will work

for food is the easiest option, you can't always choose what is going to reinforce your cat's behaviour at a given time.

For example, there is a cardboard box left out in the hall and your cat approaches it. You ask him to sit and he does

so. You mark the sit. How will you reinforce it? Well, you might give him a tasty treat but, actually, at that point in time the highest reinforcer would probably be allowing your cat to hop in the box. We don't get to choose what reinforces the animal's behaviour – only the cat at that time can decide!

The Tricks

The tricks we are going to teach you and your cat fall into three difficulty levels: easy, tricky and taxing. We definitely suggest that you start with the easy ones. Once you have the fundamentals in place, the sky really is the limit for how you build them together to create more complicated tricks. If you teach your cat those primary skills – for example, to pick something up and to hand target – there is nothing to stop you putting those skills together and teaching him to pick up your keys and bring them right to your hand.

We have also categorized them into tricks that will make your cat useful around the house, and party pieces that are show-stopping antics to help build your cat's profile.

The most important thing is that both you and your cat enjoy the training. It should be fun and rewarding for both of you, so if you or your cat feels frustrated or starts to switch off, then take a break and come back to it.

Easy Tricks

Target Training
for Cats

To get you started, let's do some simple tricks. The cool thing about teaching the basics is that the basics are actually a foundation for everything else. And, as is often the case with foundations, the stronger they are the better the other tricks will be as a result of that solid prior knowledge.

First off, **target training** for cats is a great way to start the process. Remember that we are teaching the cats to love learning. With that in mind I'm going to suggest that for these easy tricks you keep sessions to between 3–5 minutes before a substantial break. You can do around three sessions like this a day, but don't be too greedy and squeeze your cat's brain dry. Make sure, if you can help it, to finish the session before the cat asks you to stop!

Target Training for Cats

Time to train: 1 week of 3 x sessions a day (3–5 minutes per session)

Type of trick: Useful

Future application: Ask your cat to touch anything with his nose by using a Post-it note, cutting it down and fading it. Perfect for teaching cats to turn lights on and off or an alternative method for ringing the bell.

What you will need: Post-it notes, treats, clicker.

We will use the hand target later for our **retrieves** and also for our **recall**. The paper targets will come in useful for closing doors and ringing bells. Teaching an animal to target items is one of the most useful things we can teach them and we've used variations of it when moving livestock from a to b, when we ask our hens to go to bed, or when we want a cat to stand on a table to be examined by a vet.

Hand Target

1. Get a reward ready for your cat.
2. Take another reward and place it in between your middle finger and forefinger.
3. Put your open hand to the side of the cat's face – close enough that they will be able to smell the treat but not so close that they might find it a bit intimidating.

4. Mark as soon as she sniffs the treat between your fingers, or as soon as she investigates the hand.

5. Once you mark, remove your hand behind your back and use your other hand to present a reward to your clever cat.

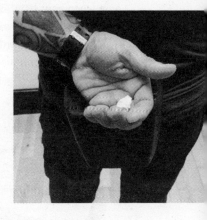

6. Repeat this about ten times or until it's clear your cat knows that she has to investigate your hand in order to earn her reward. Once this is the case, remove the lure treat from your fingers and keep playing the game.

Note: cats, being cats, they often like to mooch around during training. If a dog was to behave in this manner we would suggest they have disengaged with the training game; however, cats just tend to take their time a bit more than dogs. If you are used to training dogs but this is your first foray into cat training, remember that they train a little differently and do like to mooch.

When Millie mooched during training Jo would just let her swan about. Don't stroke too much or engage too much with your cat if she is mooching around, as she is probably just processing and investigating the environment and your tools. Use the stroking as part of the reward after a mark and allow your cat time to mooch before re-presenting your palm. Jo would wait until Millie gave her eye contact to suggest she was ready to play again before continuing with the new repetition. Over time, Millie would specifically communicate that she was ready to go again, which saved a lot of time guessing.

7. Once you have a cat that will touch your hand with her nose when your hand is presented, you can start asking with a word. Start by saying 'touch', then presenting your hand. Mark and reward the times she clearly targets your hand. Start ignoring really weak ones when the cat isn't really touching your hand properly.

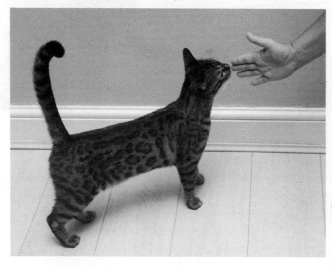

8. After you have done some repetitions and your cat is confidently touching your hand when you say 'touch', start adding a bit of distance. Put your hand out about 30 cm away from your cat so she has to actually take a few steps to touch your hand. Repeat this and, over the next few sessions, start adding more and more distractions.

9. Once the behaviour is on cue – which means that whenever you ask (and your cat hears) they come straight over and touch your hand – you can start trying to train it in other rooms in the house, and then eventually other places.

Paper Targets

To train with paper targets we would always encourage people to use Post-it notes. These are great, as they are easily and cheaply replaceable when they get covered in food or, with some species, slobber. They are also sticky, which means once the animal has the idea we can start moving them away from the hand.

1. Get a Post-it note and drag a little bit of your cat's food over it so that it smells of food.

2. Present the Post-it note to the side of your cat's face like you did previously with your outstretched palm. Instead of putting the Post-it note in your palm (as your cat will likely just target the palm as he has learnt previously), put the Post-it between your fingers so that it hangs down. Your hand can remain palm downwards like a ceiling to the Post-it note.

3. Mark and reward your cat as soon as he touches the Post-it note with his nose, or as soon as he investigates it. Just like with your hand, move the Post-it note away and behind your back once your cat has done it correctly and you are rewarding him.
4. After he has finished mooching and seems up for more, re-present the Post-it and go again. Get at least five successful repetitions out of the way before you rip up that Post-it note and grab a clean, non-smelly one to practise with.
5. Once you've had a few successful repetitions on the clean note, you want to increase the strength of the behaviour. What we mean by this is that we want the cat to really put pressure with his nose on the target rather than just lightly touch it. In order to be clear with your feline friend, we will start marking and reinforcing the targets only when the force of his cat nose moves the Post-it note.
6. When this is reliable, we can give the behaviour a name. We usually use the name 'target' to explain to your cat you want him to touch a target and not your hand. Say 'target' each time prior to presenting the target for your cat to touch.

7. Once your cat is doing this and you have practised over a few sessions, then start placing the targets away from your hand and on the wall. To start with, you will want to be right next to the wall with your cat so that the context is really similar to when the Post-it was hanging from your hand. It might be that a little prompting is necessary. If that is the case – and after saying 'target' and putting the Post-it on the wall your cat stares at you blankly – then feel free to give him more information by touching the Post-it with your finger a few times to point him in the right direction.

8. After a fair few successful repetitions (we work by the rule that we will only move to the next step if the cat is confidently performing the behaviour reliably enough that we would bet £50 that they will succeed all of the next five repetitions), start adding more and more distance until upon the word 'target' your cat will move from where he is to the Post-it on the wall and touch it with his nose.

9. It's probably worth starting close and easy when you move the Post-it onto the floor as well, so you are right there to prompt if necessary and to mark and reward immediately, as the target being on the floor might feel a little different to it being at eye height to the cat.

10. After this behaviour is reliable, try mixing up the targets. Lids of baby food cups and milk lids make great targets. If you want to introduce a new target, start again at the beginning of this process. Each time your cat learns a new target, the next target will be even easier to teach!

Recall

Time to train: 2 weeks of 1 x session a day
Type of trick: Useful
Application: Using different cues for the same trick but in a different context is a great skill to learn but recall is so important and useful as well
What you will need: A whistle, a clicker, a cat and some scrummy cat treats

Recall to a whistle will feel pretty easy after the targets. Effectively all we are really doing is adding a new cue (a whistle) and adding speed and distance to a hand target. Yep, we are going to teach a recall to the sound of a whistle so your cat will perform a hand touch. Calling your cat in from hunting or prowling their territory will never be the same again!

1. First off, we need to desensitize your cat to the sound of a whistle. The whistle is going to be quite loud (as you will want to use it to call her in from further afield) and maybe a new and scary noise for your cat. So, first off, although the noise might be a bit uncomfortable, we will pair it with something good to ensure your cat loves it before using it in training. For a week we want you to whistle before breakfast, dinner and playtime, and

before you give her a treat outside of the training context (where you use a marker). By the end of the week your cat should absolutely love the sound of the whistle.

2. Next we are going to teach you how to put a new cue (a word to ask the cat to perform the act of touching your hand) to a behaviour (touching your hand with her nose), which she has already nailed with an old cue (the word 'touch').

   • First whistle with your whistle.
   • Then outstretch your palm for her to touch.

- Then say 'touch'.
- As soon as she performs her nose-target, mark and reward her.

3. You are going to repeat the above process multiple times. At some point you will notice that your cat starts to do what is known as 'jumping the prompt'. That means, upon hearing the whistle, she will go to touch your hand before the cue 'touch' has been given. At this point, you can stop using the word 'touch' when you recall her.

4. The whole point of a recall is that it's fast and furious. To get it quickly we need your cat to be really, really keen on the sound. She needs to be highly motivated to come to your hand when she hears it. With that in mind, after the previous stage on close and structured training sessions, we are going to practise this in a slightly different way. Rather than having training sessions for this one, you are only going to practise it three times a day. The first time will be for half her breakfast and the third time will be for half her dinner.

5. At some point – at a different time – each day, you will whistle the cat. After the cat has come and offered a hand touch, you will give her an extra meal, but this meal will be full of all her absolutely favourite things. When you first start, it might be a great idea to cook up a chicken at the beginning of the week and saw off chunks to give as whistle-touch rewards each day.

6. After a week of this, don't forget to continue to reward your cat for their recall-touch when you take the training into different rooms and over further distances, and then, when it's reliable, in the house – that's right: take it outside! Keep the value of the rewards really, really high, as this is arguably the most important training you'll do and could even save your cat's life.

Teaching Your Cat to Sit

Time to train: 1 week of 2 x sessions a day (3–5 minutes per session)

Type of trick: Useful/party piece

Application: Now you have learnt how to train your cat to sit, have a go at writing your own plan for how to teach her to stand on cue, too

What you will need: To begin you will just need some rewards, a marker and your cat. For best results start in your training space

1. Take a reward between your forefinger and thumb and move it to the side of your cat's face so they can smell it.

2. Once they've locked onto the scent of the reward, move the reward up above their head and slightly behind them so the cat has to either move backwards or put their behind down for them to get to the treat.

3. As soon as the back end of the cat has lowered, mark and reward your cat.
4. Repeat this four times and then, on the fifth, hold the treat there until the cat's bottom hits the surface and the cat is in a sitting position.

Once they have eaten their treat, if they have remained in the sit then feed them another reward. It's great to reinforce the cat for maintaining the position, as it will make it stronger. After a few treats in the sit, if the cat still hasn't got up, feed and stroke them. Stroking the cat will reward her for her posture and at the same time it will prompt her to get up.

5. As soon as the cat is on four feet, get a new lure out
    and hold it above the cat's head for a sit again. Repeat
    it numerous times until the cat is popping into that
    sit posture quickly every time she sees your hand move
    up there.

6. When the sit behaviour is reliable with the hand gesture,
    we will bring in a word to ask the cat to do it. The key
    here is to say the word FIRST: 'Sit!' Then give your cat
    the hand gesture. This way the word predicts the gestures
    happening and, in the end, the cat will respond to the
    word 'sit' rather than waiting for the hand gesture.

7. Now nice the test: ask 'sit' without any hand gesture x 3.
    If she gets all three right, you're ready for distractions. If
    not, just keep practising.

Beg

Time to train: 2 weeks of 2 x sessions a day (3–5 minutes per session)
Type of trick: Party piece
Application: Once he has nailed the beg position you can attempt challenging your cat to #balancebeg. (Planking went viral, then the mannequin challenge – let's see if getting cats to balance-beg in strange places might be the next big internet craze!)
What you will need: Somewhere solid for your cat to balance, a clicker, some treats and a clever cat

This is a great little party trick and will most definitely earn you kitty kudos on Instagram. It's also great for improving balance and core strength – not that it's likely your cat will need a helping paw in this department!

1. Take a treat and ask for a sit.

2. Offer treat to your cat for sitting while she is in position.
3. Now take a treat between your fingers and offer it to your cat's nose.
4. Just as she reaches for it pull it straight up as if she were a puppet and the treat was attached to her string.

5. For the first five repetitions mark and then reward when your cat reaches up.
6. For the next five repetitions your cat needs to pull at least one paw off the surface she is sitting on to earn a mark and a reward.

7. After you have done this five times, repeat again, but this time you're waiting for two paws to leave the surface. It might be that you need to pull the treat a little bit higher and backwards to get two paws up. At any point she breaks her sit, start again. It is important she learns to use the sitting position to balance her into the beg or she will be standing on two back legs, which isn't very good for cats' legs!

8. Once you are getting a nice beg position each and every time you present your moving lure to your cat, you are going to shake things up a bit and lose the treat in your hand. Instead, lure your cat up with an empty hand and then reward her in position with the other hand.

9. To start bringing in a bit of balance we recommend that you feed three treats: one, then two, then three – one after another while your cat is in the beg – then mark and give her a treat as well.

Start to tidy up that lure as you bring in your cue word. That means for the next session you will say 'beg', then use an empty hand slightly away from her face in an upward movement to gesture what you want her to do. It might be that you can't go from a full motion with an empty hand to suddenly just pointing the hand up. If your cat struggles to understand that you are cueing the beg, then instead start with a three-quarter gesture, then a half gesture, then a partial gesture, before asking the cat simply by the word and a small upward gesture.

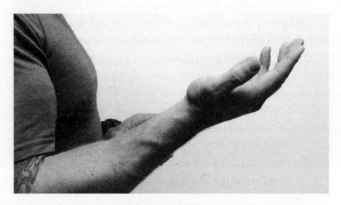

10. Once your cat understands that on the word 'beg' she has to take this position, then you can start working in different rooms and eventually new places.

Down

Time to train: 1 week of 2 x sessions a day (3–5 minutes per session)

Type of trick: Useful/party piece

Application: There are lots of add-ons to the down – try teaching a 'guilty' expression (head on paws), a lay flat or even try adding the target and the down together to teach a 'go to bed'

What you will need: A marker, a cat, plenty of treats and a bit of patience

Teaching your cat to down as well as sit is useful and will help him to relax when you ask. It will also be important in some of the more complicated tricks later, such as the hypnotize trick. Because cats are much smaller than dogs, it can be hard to lure them into the down. With that in mind, you will need to sit on the floor with your legs stretched out straight in front for this lesson.

1. First ask your cat to sit so they are facing your knee and your leg is running like a road in front of them.

2. Feed the cat for going into the sit by arching up your leg and placing a treat in your fingers under your knee. The cat will need to reach in to collect his prize.

3. Ask him to sit again. This time lower the arch of your knee a little so your cat has to bend his head low to receive his treat. Repeat this a few times. If your cat gets out of his sit, simply remove the food and ask for the sit again.

4. Once your cat is reaching with his head low in the sit to get the treat from under your leg, ask your cat into a sit again. This time keep the bridge of your leg really low. It needs to be just high enough so that it's like a tunnel for your cat. Stick your arm through and reach up so your cat can bend in his sit to sniff it, then pull it down under the bridge of your leg to pull him down. This time, only mark and reward when he snuffles into a semi-down to collect his treat. Repeat this over a couple of sessions until he is moving easily into the down.

Note: if you aren't that flexible and struggle training on the floor, then you can attempt the same logic without the tunnel. So, ask for the sit and reward lower and lower and lower, eventually coaxing the cat to go right down with the chest touching the floor. Make sure that the treat disappears and you start each repetition again if your cat gets up from the sit during this part.

5. Once your cat is moving easily from sit to down, and you are no longer feeding under your knee, you can start to remove the lure. So, you will simply pretend you have food in your hand and lure your cat into position with an empty hand. If you try this multiple times and it just isn't working, then go back a step and get the behaviour stronger with the food still in the hand.

6. Once your cat is working from an empty lure and following the hand gesture into a down position, start pointing instead of holding your hand like you have a treat in it. Point at the floor by pointing but still dragging your point down the air for a little run, then mark and reward the cat's position when he gets it right.

7. Next, change that gesture so you aren't moving your hand down the air at all. You are just pointing and your cat is taking the right position.

8. Once this is reliable you can bring in the cue word. We usually use the word 'down' for this position. As with the sit, it is important that the cat knows what they are doing (exactly what position they are expected to hold:

chest on floor) before you bring in the word. Only bring in the word if you're convinced that when you say it and then point, your cat will get it right. Now have a little practice.

9. Now test your cat by doing a whistle, hand touch, followed by a sit, followed by a target to a Post-it note, then ask for the down. Practise these four cued behaviours in different orders during a single training session to ensure your cat truly understands what you are asking him to do.

A note on timings

Please don't worry if your cat is slower to pick up tricks than the timeframes we're using in the book. All cats are individuals and these are only rough guides. Like us, they may be more up for it some days than others, they may not be in the mood, or may seem to have taken one step forwards and two steps back. That's all part of the process. Please keep in mind that this should be fun for both of you. If you find yourself overly frustrated by your cat's progress, then it's possible that tricks just aren't meant to be part of your relationship. In which case, use the techniques you have learnt to enjoy playing and giving your cat the attention they relish.

Even if your cat does pick up some elements quickly, it won't be one long straight road. Remember that we learn more from the bits the cats find hard than the bits they find easy. Always know when to take a break to think about what you need to do.

Strengthening the Behaviour and Building on Distractions and Duration

When you watch some trainers with their animals, all the things they are asking for seem so polished! Training (like a hand touch, sit, down or beg) can look slick and professional, but to get it like that there are some additional steps.

First off you can start using distractions to add duration and strength to your behaviour. Start by asking for a behaviour – let's say, on this occasion, you have asked for a sit, then, just as your cat sits, make micro-movements with your other hand in her periphery to distract her. To start this we are literally talking about one microsecond of a finger wiggle. If you cat stays in the sit then feed, feed, feed. Once your cat 'gets' that their job is to stay in the sit or down, or with their nose on your hand, during these gentle distractions, you can begin other, harder distractions. These may include you doing a spin or a little tap dance – or, as you get more advanced, they may include a new person entering the training room, or even a fellow pet.

As the behaviours you are training get stronger and stronger, you can use the reward as a distraction as well. So, try asking for a position: let's say you have asked your cat for a down. Then pop the reward just in front of her. If she remains in the down, mark and release her onto the reward. If she breaks her position, remove the reward.

As time goes on, and you develop your really stable sit, down, beg and touch behaviour with distraction, you may wish to add longer duration. That means you want your cat to stay in the position until told otherwise. For this I usually start to bring in a *release* cue as well.

Ask for a position – for example, a beg. If you are attempting a long goal, such as five full minutes in the beg, stick your timer on. Reward the cat in the position every thirty seconds on the first go. Then, at ten minutes, mark and use your release word (we use 'OK', but other common release words include 'release', 'free' and 'go'). After your release cue, feed your cat away from where they have been lying, sitting

More
Challenging
Tricks

More Challenging Tricks

So now your cat is getting to grips with the process of learning and you are becoming quite the cat-wrangling professional – let's step it up a gear. The following tricks are a mix of party pieces that will start to rack up the views on YouTube, as well as things that will genuinely make your life better as a cat owner.

Heel

Time to train: 2 weeks of 3 sessions a day (3–5 minutes per session)

Type of trick: Useful/party piece

Application: Teaching cats to target bits of your body is a great training skill. Why not have a go at teaching a chin target on your leg (very cute) or a paw target on your hand (high five)

What you will need: A marker, Post-it notes, treats

Heel work is something cats are naturally good at. As a cat owner you won't be shocked at hearing this, given the amount of near misses you've had with a hot coffee or a carefully constructed platform cake as you walk through the kitchen trying to get the cat OUT of heel position!

The heel position definitely looks great, though – and if you train it properly you can even attempt heel work to music. That's right: *Britain's Got Talent* beware! Additionally, it can be really useful if you have a house cat who is seldom given the chance to get out, or if you want to start taking your cat to new places but don't fancy being pulled around the park by a cat on a lead.

1. Take a treat in your hand. For this first bit we need to teach you to do what is, in the training world, called a 'crane drop', and to do this we need you to start training in the training room but without your cat. Start by crouching or kneeling on the floor (you can kneel on

a cushion if you want to be extra comfortable). Get a nice, small and salient reward (something like a cube of chicken will work well). Take the reward and hold it in between your fingers so all of your fingertips are holding it (like the beak of a bird). Arch your hand and release the food directly downwards like one of the mini-cranes inside toy-grabber machines.

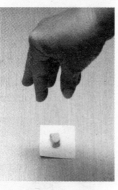

2. Practise holding and dropping the little cubes. Get a Post-it note and place it on the floor. Now practise dropping it onto the Post-it. Once you can get five in a row on target, stand up and go again.

3. Once you have five standing targets in a row, place a number of Post-its in a path, as if each Post-it was a paw-print track to the exit of the room. Start at one end of the track and practise craning the food onto the targets on each Post-it. Keep practising until you can do a whole run of the path with each piece of reward hitting a target point. Once you can do that, you are ready for your feline friend to join you.

4. Get a Post-it and stick it to the side of your calf. Stand by the sofa or by a wall so there is just room for the cat to stand straight, partitioned between you and the wall. For this training we are going to aim high and go for a formal Crufts-style heel position. Mark and reward your cat for touching the target on your leg. Mark and reward her via a crane drop, landing directly down in front of her, ten times in a row when her nose hits the target on your calf. This is her heel position, and the wall or sofa will hold her straight, so she can get used to it. On this first session, just mark and reward the position. Don't worry about movement until she is nailing position.

5. Start by moving one leg forward once she touches the target. Target touched = that leg forward. Then, when she touches that forward leg, mark and reward. Once she is clearly coming into position when you stand there, stand somewhere else in the room and try again.

6. Your next stage is to remove the target. To do this you are first going to rip the target in half and keep practising. Then in half again, and keep going until the cat is touching a small target instead of a big square.

7. Now bring in the verbal cue – the word you will use to call your cat in. We use 'close', although common cues for heel are 'heel', 'snug' and 'tight'. Say 'close', then wait for the nose-touch; step one foot forward, get a second nose-touch, then mark at reward. Then repeat this until there is no doubt that your cat understands that she needs to move into this spot and stay there touching your leg to earn her reward.

8. Once she gets that 'close' means 'target the leg', try to give it a go without a target at all. Try by asking her 'close' without the target present at all. Mark and give her a proper little jackpot each time she is able to go into heel on cue without a target.

9. Once the cat is clearly finding position easily on cue, and doesn't mind sticking with that leg as it moves forward, you can start using actual distance. As soon as you do this, the rules change. Start walking very slowly and mark and crane drop each time she touches your leg. Repeat this and walk very slowly. It doesn't matter at this stage that your cat is very likely stopping and picking up the crane-dropped chicken as she goes – just stop, wait for her to return by herself and nose-target your leg.

10. The rest is easy sailing from here. Simply add distance. So, walk from one point to the door. Call your cat into close, then mark and crane drop each time she tries to nose-touch you. Pay her for each and every attempt.

11. Once you have practised this for quite a few sessions, and your cat should be pretty reliable, you

should see your cat's nose staying close to your leg in a heel position for longer and longer. Now use a cue to get your cat into heel command. Walk from one side of the room to the next but only crane down five treats, regardless of her nose. This should make for longer and better nose-touches.

12. Over the next few sessions, work on speed of walking and cutting down how many treats she has on the walk across the room so that it's not excessive.

13. Keep practising and slowly, slowly, reduce how many treats she is having for remaining in the heel.

14. If you think your cat has nailed it, start practising the training in different areas, in different parts of the house, and then eventually anywhere you like! Even if your close cue is really reliable, don't use it by the side of main roads or any place that could result in your cat being somewhere risky or dangerous.

Ring the Bell for Dinner

Type of trick: YouTube showstopper

Application: Desensitizing your cat to new sounds can help him grow in confidence around new things generally. Now he knows how to press a button, why not teach him to turn the lamp on and off on cue, or even switch the music on and off on the stereo!

What you will need: A dinner bell, a marker, treats, a table and chairs

There is a very famous and popular YouTube clip of two cats sitting at a table, ringing bells for their owners to place food on their plates. This trick is pretty simple to teach and achieving showstopping quality from it is all about the set-up.

While initially we are going to train your cat to press a dinner bell, eventually we will train him to sit at the dinner table on a chair and press it. The table can be set like a feast if you really want to impress.

Initial set-up for training: you will need a dinner bell, a marker and something to reinforce your cat for session one. For session two you will also require a table and chairs. For session three you'll need the table set up how you wish for the final show as well.

Set your training room so the bell is in the middle of the floor. There are two ways to train this and it depends if you

are training the trick from scratch but also if you want a paw target or a nose target. I prefer to teach a paw target with the dinner bell, as, in my opinion, it looks way more impressive. If you want to use a nose target then simply desensitize the bell as per below, attach a Post-it to the bell and slowly, over successful repetitions of the cat nose-targeting the bell for it to ring, break the Post-it into smaller and smaller targets until there is no target and, upon the cue 'ring', the cat rings. After that, skip to step 6 on page 82 and teach your cat to do it on a chair.

Just like the whistle, to begin we need to desensitize the bell. Ring the bell and feed a treat. Start with the bell a fair distance from your cat and move it closer and closer over the session. If your cat is happy to hang out, ring the bell next to them and collect a treat off the bell, then you are ready to begin the training.

1. To teach the paw target for this one, all you need to do is show your cat a few bits of food going on the floor. Quickly cover the food by holding the bell over the food and hold the bell down.

2. Your cat will investigate in an attempt to get to the food. Wait for him to scratch the bell before marking and rewarding by lifting the bell for your cat to get all the treats. Repeat this.

3. As soon as your cat is at a point where he is straight on the bell as soon as it gets placed on the floor, repeat, but this time do not move the bell so the cat gets the treat from under it. Instead, mark the scratch but then feed the cat from your stash. Repeat this until the cat definitely understands what is getting them the reward.

4. Once the cat is going straight into the paw scratch of the bell, remove the luring treats from under the bell and keep going.

5. Then start picking the bell up between repetitions and placing the bell down as a sign to the cat to paw now. Repeat until your cat is really, really confident with this game.

OK – so now it's time to add in the props. Keep the table empty to begin with – no distractions. Simply have a plate

in front of where you want your cat to sit. Lure your cat up onto the chair with the promise of a treat.

We recommend that, to begin with, you now do a whole session of luring the cat up onto the chair and feeding on the chair – this will get the cat used to being on the chair and making it a nice place to be. Remember to choose a chair you won't mind the cat frequently using as, after this training, he will always think of this chair as a great place to be. If your cat is eager to climb up onto the chair at the mere hint of a food reward, then great. You are ready for the next bit.

6. First hold the bell out to the cat on the chair. Hold it in the same position as if you were asking for his paw and mark and reward when he hits it. Each time he hits it, reward him by putting a reward on the dinner plate in front of him and remove the bell. Re-present the bell each repetition, then mark the target and feed on the plate.

7. At some point sooner or later this will get a bit easier. So, start raising the bell little increment by little increment until your cat can reach the bell on the table. Slowly move your hand away as well, bit by bit, until the cat is repeatedly ringing the bell on the table and you are repeatedly rewarding him on the plate.

8. It's time for the props. I wouldn't use real bits and bobs – these cats are yet to have a self-control super-ability, so set them up to succeed.

9. Use fake food and bring it in from a great distance away, so as not to distract our bell ringer. Then move it closer and closer to the bell each session until the table is set up as you wish. And hey presto! Your cats are ready for an all-time classic YouTube video of the cats pressing the bell!

Hypnotize

Training time: 2 weeks of 3 x sessions of 5 minutes a day
Type of trick: Instagram crowd pleaser
Application: This trick is all about putting two behaviours together and making it seem to the viewer like one thing is happening when in fact it's something else. Use these acting skills to teach your cat other magic tricks, such as 'Bang Bang (You're Dead)'
What you will need: A marker, treats

The hypnotize trick seems to be particularly well received when dogs do it on social media – so just imagine that this is your cat instead! And if you're not mad about posting videos online, it is still a super-fun hoax to play with your friends when they come over.

1. Ask your cat to go into the down position. If she struggles then you need to take a step back in time and revisit the foundation work earlier in the book.

2. Now you are going to reward your cat at the shoulder. So when the chest hits the floor, show your cat the reward and move it in a quarter circle so they have to turn their face

around to eat near their shoulder. What happens when you do this is that they will start to lean to that side. Mark any leaning whatsoever.

3. Repeat this until it's comfortable and easy for your feline friend.

4. The next step is to pull the treat very slightly over the top of the shoulder blade. The cat then has to lean even further onto her side in order to get that treat. Mark at the furthest point of leaning that you think you'll get to.

Repeat this ten times. Often what happens during this stage is that the cat will actually flop onto her side during reps because it's more comfortable to do so. If she does this, jackpot her – give her a whole load of treats and fuss.

5. Once the cat is leaning further each time, start pulling the reward over her head and to the front of her face, so she is on her side with her head resting. It is important that we reward a comfortable posture, as we want the cat to be able to hold it and hold it still.

6. Repeat this over a couple of sessions until it's clear the cat knows to flop onto her side when the treat comes to her shoulder.

7. Part two of this trick involves a very basic eye-contact aspect as well. To do this, start showing the treat to the cat in the down position, then raise the treat to your eyes. You can bring in the cue straight away for this one, so: down say, 'Look into my eyes, my eyes, my eyes' treat on your nose mark and reward. Then get out a second treat and start saying, 'Sleep', then take the treat to the shoulder. Practise in two parts like this until both parts are very fluid.

8. Now put them together. Ask for the down then say, 'Look into my eyes …' treat on the nose then pull treat onto the shoulder of the cat as you say, 'Now sleep' mark and reward.

9. Over time you can gradually add duration to your lay flat position. So each time you practise, add on a quarter of a second before giving the reward. Once you get up to one second, feed at one second, then again at two seconds, then again at three. You need mark only once (not each reward); as long as kitty stays in her position you can keep feeding.

10. Then start adding time between the treats. Reward at two, six, ten seconds in the down. Draw this out until on the word 'sleep' your cat stays down and out for a full ten seconds.

Leg Weaves

Training time: 3 weeks of 3 x sessions, 5 minutes a day

Type of trick: A trick Facebook will go wild for

Application: Nailed the leg weaves? Then it's time to teach your cat to weave other things too. Most hilarious on fence poles or when workmen have left out cones. Additionally, you can break this trick down and teach the leg wrap as an extra trick. Teaching a wraparound means you can also add distance and send your cat around other objects on cue

What you will need: A marker, treats, traffic cones

1. Take a treat and stand with your legs in an upside-down V but with one side angled slightly ahead of the other.
2. Use the treat to lure your cat-training veteran through the arch. Wrap him around your leg so that he comes out to the front of you again for the treat. Now take a step

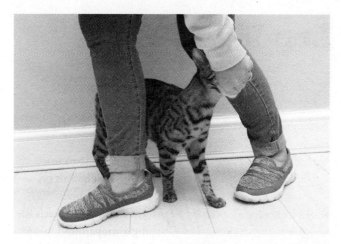

forward to angle the second side of the V in front of the first side and go again.

3. Repeat these two parts in sequence. It can be very slow to start with, but that's fine, as the speed can come later.

4. Once your cat seems really fluid you're going to start the age-old process you have come to know well: fading that lure.

5. In the next session, start by wrapping your cat around leg one, mark at the front and reward for leg two, but use an empty hand. So, still lure him, just without the food. Then, for the next go, no food in the first leg and additionally try putting your hand down to your side on the outside of your leg instead of pulling your cat through with your treat. On the second leg of this go, repeat the process without placing your hand through your legs to lure.

If this is successful, practise these four moves in sequence up and down your training space, or on the spot if you haven't got room. You want to nail this part of the process so that it is really smooth.

6. Right, next up we are going to fade the lure even more. This time, place your legs in an upside-down V and wait until your cat guesses by moving at all to the entrance. As soon as they do this off their own bat, then place your lure hand out front, where you would give the treat. Mark as they pass through your legs, then give them a reward and go again.

7. When this is fluid, you can start getting your cat to do two legs before marking and rewarding. Open the upside-down V and wait for your cat to enter; as they wrap, make a diagonal lure and adjust your legs so that they wrap around the next leg before marking and rewarding. Practise this until it's really fluent and hopefully getting faster too! At this point bring in the cue 'weave' as you open your upside-down V ready to start.

8. Over the next few weeks start increasing the pace each day and reducing the lure. When your cat is fast and sure-footed, start asking for four-leg weaves prior to marking and rewarding. Build up and up until your cat will weave on one cue until you mark.

9. Place your phone on a low stool at cat-head height for awesome social media footage. You can even introduce props!

Wipe Feet

Time to training: 2 weeks of 3–5 sessions a day, 2 minutes
   a pop
Type of trick: Very useful and will make all the visitors to
   your home laugh
Application: Scratching on cue can help if you want to train
   'take toys out of a box' on cue or if you want to teach her
   to use a scratch post
What you will need: A doormat, some treats

1. Lift up the doormat you want to use and let your cat see
    you sprinkle a little mixture of delights under the mat.

2. Hold the mat down with your feet but bend down
    so that your cat isn't expected to work under your
    towering height.

3. If she struggled then keep lifting the mat a little so she can smell the treats below.

4. As soon as she scratches, mark and then lift the mat for her to help herself to the under-mat buffet.

5. Repeat this process five times.

6. Then repeat but this time have a treat ready in your hand and, when she has scratched, mark and feed from your hand, leaving the buffet below the mat.

7. Repeat this five times and on the sixth go allow her to have the treats under the mat.

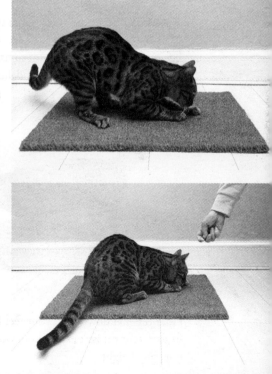

8. In your next session, start with fewer treats under the mat and, after your first five repetitions, remove the treats entirely.

9. This time wait for your cat to guess that they need to scratch to be marked and get their reward. Be patient and have faith in your flighty feline friend. She may want to mooch around a little first but she will get there!

10. Once she has understood that scratching the mat is what is getting her the reward, then add your cue word. Say 'wipe your feet' as she approaches the mat and then mark and reward her for doing so.

11. After this you can begin stepping away from the mat yourself and adding more and more distance and then sending your cat onto the mat to wipe her feet.

12. This is such a cool one for a cat to learn, and gone are the days when cats and white sofas were mutually exclusive.

Complex Tricks

Wow! You have exceeded yourself to have stalked so easily through the last two levels, and now there is absolutely no pussyfooting around. You're cohabiting with a trick-cat ninja. With this in mind, the last two tricks are designed to teach you some particulars that can be used when designing other tricks. What that means is that both these tricks have links that make a chain. We will explain how to train each of the following links: pick up and hold; carry to me; touch my hand with an object still in your mouth; drop object; jump onto a marker; take a position at a distance, and remain despite distraction until released. And also go through putting them together to make two example chains. This means that you could lift out any of the behaviour links and slot them into new chains – like lifting the chicken out of a Caesar salad and replacing it with salmon for an alternative meal.

Training Cats to Use Their Mouths

Overall training time: 6 weeks of 3 x training sessions per day of around 5 minutes

Application: The list is endless – retrieve any item, search and retrieve, hold any item, drop anything when asked. Use this training to perfect your cat's best 'hold a sign in their mouth' expression, as well as their 'ringing phone retrieve', or even teach a dumbbell retrieve and combine it with a heel and a jump to impress obedience judges and prove that if dogs can do it, cats can too!

What you will need: Clicker, various items for your cat to hold.

The Hold

The hold is the first bit we train. Just like dogs, cats are predators and use their mouths to catch and kill and then eat things. This means that asking them to put things in their mouths isn't quite as much of a foreign concept as it may seem.

1. Start by choosing an item that your cat won't find unpleasant to put in their mouth. You can use a toy here but I prefer to blur the lines of what's a toy and what isn't straightaway, so a ribbon or a child's toy or even a small paint roller does the trick. If you are

aiming for the cat to get their collar, then you can start working with a collar. If you want your cat to retrieve the mobile phone, then weave a toggle to go on the phone and start with the toggle.

2. Hold out the item and mark and reward each time your cat investigates it. The first ten treats are for any level of investigation. Remember to hide the item behind your back each time before re-presenting it for the next trial.

3. Now hold off for your cat to put their mouth on the item. Mouth-touching the item is what gets the mark and the reward. Be clear. If the cat gets too many wrong and appears to lose interest, go back to simply marking investigation for a few more repetitions before moving on.

4. Now start holding off the clicker for your cat to open their mouth on the collar or on the toggle. Mark and reward any teeth action.

5. Build from here, and remember that you can use this process to get your cat to essentially hold anything.

6. Repeat this and build up until your cat is opening their mouth on the item.

7. Once the cat is clearly taking the item in his mouth, add a little bit of resistance with two fingers. This should cause the cat to bite down harder. Mark and reward that and repeat until the bite is hard.

8. This time present the item lower, so the cat has to bend their head down to grab the item. In doing so, they will lift the item. Mark the lift and be there to take the item before it falls. If at any stage an item falls on the floor,

103

do not mark and
reward. Instead,
re-present the
item and go for
another repetition.

9. Lower the item
each time you are
confident your cat
has got the idea
of picking up the
item from a height all the way until he is picking it up
off the floor for you to catch.

10. Once you have got to this stage, a well-deserved pat on
the back along with a pat on the cat is deserved. Make
sure you are still breaking frequently, so your cat doesn't
suffer with training fatigue.

11. It's time to bring in the cue, so each time you present the
item on the floor, say, 'Hold the XXX' and then mark
and reward the pick-up five times before moving on.

12. Now that your
cat is picking up
the item, you
need to wait a
little microsecond
before you mark,
so he is picking
up and then
holding the item.
Keep working on
this, along with
distractions. If you
take a look at the
previous section

in this book, about strengthening behaviours, then we would suggest you follow that with this part of the trick. If you can get your cat to hold items on cue with distractions then that will serve you really well for further tricks.

Touch My Hand with the Item in Your Mouth

1. Ask your cat to hold the item you have been training with. Let's say, for the sake of an example, he is holding the phone by the toggle.
2. Once he has lifted and held it, ask him to 'touch' and place out your hand.
3. Use the marker as soon as your cat touches your hand and you collect the item.

4. Mark and reward.
5. If he drops the item that is meant to touch the hand, simply pick it back up without marking or rewarding and go again. If he gets five wrong in a row, you need to work harder at the hold.
6. Once this is nailed and reliable, start adding distance.
7. To do this, simply place the item slightly further and further away each rep.
8. If you are teaching a ringing phone or something similar, now is the time to add your cue. Place the item away and ring the phone, followed by sending the cat on to collect it. If the cat is a little worried about the phone, then practise the desensitization as we did with the whistle. So, simply ring the phone by the dinner bowl before dinner every day for a week.

9. Once the cat is picking up, carrying and placing in your hand, then you are onto a winner.
10. If you fancy training your cat to hold something and take a position (for example, 'hold a sign' but take a beg position), then train that in exactly the same way. Ask the cat to hold the item, then ask for the beg. If they drop the item or break position, start again. Make sure both links in this chain are super strong before putting them together, though.

So now you have it. You can send your cat on to pick things up. Pretty soon he will be applying to be an assistance cat!

Cat on the Dog (or Skateboard)

Training time: 8 weeks of 5 x sessions of 5–7 minutes a day

Type of trick: The ultimate in YouTube viral video material

Applications: For our party piece on the show, we trained Hannah to teach River, the beautiful Bengal cat, to ride Moss, the chilled Labrador. The trick itself is hardcore but if you want to train your cat to jump into a cat basket on a bike and ride in it or leap on a skateboard, it's all pretty much the same with a few ingredients swapped about

What you will need: A marker, treats, a dog saddle and/or skateboard

1. Start by marking and rewarding any interest in the item on which you want the cat to position themselves. If any of you are mad enough to think about training the cat to ride some other animal, then you will need a saddle and you will need the saddle to be off the riding animal for the initial training.

2. For the first few sessions we will work paw by paw. Remember that if we build strong foundations then you can apply these separate links into other chains.

3. Mark and reward one paw on the saddle then, once this is easy, go for two paws, then three and then four. If you are teaching the skateboard trick, only teach three on.

4. Now the secret to this lies in the reward placement. Ensure the treat is placed in a position that also acts as a lure to get kitty into the correct position – so that might be held out in your hand above the front of the saddle or even on the saddle.

Repeat this until your cat is walking straight in and up onto the saddle.

5. Now choose your position. As we were on such a short timeframe, we were happy for River to stay how he found himself most comfortable, which was in a sit.

6. You may want your cat to beg when in the cat basket or on the dog – or pony. This is fine, but now is the time to start practising the mount on the floor and then take position. If you are training the skateboard, now is the time to train the cat to kick off. Do this by getting two feet on with you holding the

109

front, then letting go for the third leg to get on. Mark
only when the skateboard moves. Keep practising this
and, soon enough, the cat will start repeating by shifting
weight and pushing to make the skateboard move.

7. Place the saddle on the arm of the chair once the position
   is strong on the saddle and work from scratch (one paw
   on, two paws, etc.), before then working through all the
   stages to strengthen the behaviour from the previous
   section on page 70.

8. Once your cat is happily taking position on the saddle or
   item on the arm of the sofa, add your cue. Hannah used
   'River, ride' and pointed to the saddle.

9. Now in place, you need to train the other dynamic. If
   you're training your cat to ride another animal, they need
   to be taught four things: down stay; stand; recall to hand
   touch; walk steady.

10. Ask your carrier to go into a down. Ask the cat to ride. Ask the cat to take the position. Mark and reward on the saddle repeatedly. Really jackpot your cat for being so brave, and don't forget to reinforce your carrier's beautiful behaviour as well.

11. Practise this again and again. Keep your cat on there and strengthen that behaviour with both distance and duration as above.

12. Now ask the carrier to stand. To start with, to encourage your cat, we will lower what we are asking for, so mark and reward your cat for standing up against (two paws up) on the carrier or anything remotely like feet on the saddle. You could drop in an additional step and have your cat on the sofa arm and getting onto the saddle from there. That can sometimes build confidence before asking him to leap from the floor. If your 'Tom' is

finding it tough, then this is a good step to make it a bit easier first.

13. Work up to your cat jumping on, then feed. Ask for the position, feed again, then release with your release cue.

14. Repeat and repeat and then, yet again, carry out the training in the strengthening behaviour section to ensure the position on the upright carrier is really strong.

15. Now comes movement. Make sure the carrier is really slow to start. Be there and reward each and every step to begin with, then slowly start marking each two and then three and then four steps.

16. When your cat has rocked this part, start placing your carrier in a stay and asking your cat to ride. Ask them into position and then recall your steed steadily to you. If your cat breaks position or jumps off, simply start again from scratch.

Out and About with Your New Trick Cat

Did you know that the ancient Egyptians used to worship cats? Well, since working through this book has it become clear why they might have done this? Cats are absolutely mind-blowing and smart to boot. You should be feeling over the moon with what you have achieved. Remember, though, the journey isn't over. You can either take the components from these tricks to build new ones and keep up the good work or else attempt to get your cat to perform these tricks in new and different places. Take it steady and remember to always ensure you and your cat are enjoying yourselves.

Good luck and happy training!

Acknowledgements

First and foremost: Millie the little Bengal. Thank you for inspiring us to learn about the feline brain.

It's always hard to write an acknowledgements section, as we are privileged in our life to receive opportunities, help and love from so many. Christina, Chris, Charlee, Marcus, Brandon, Izzy and Millie: without your laughter and love we wouldn't get through our completely unrealistic schedule, let alone stay sane.

Santino – thanks for making this adventure extra special. Filming with a baby was something most people thought would be impossible, however, you laughed when most babies cried and definitely made the filming more exciting! Ian (Dad) – you inspire us daily, and even though we are far apart we thought of you every time we omitted a needless word. Jo – for your love, skill and commitment looking after the dogs when we take on projects like this. Our support trainers: Dean Nicolas, Adrienne Critchlow, Bryony Neve, Veronica Spinkova, Lauren Watts, Alison Mercer, Emma Riedlinger and Kate Mallatratt. Also, we want to thank Hannah and River: you guys rock!

Plimsoll – thank you so much for helping us get the positive animal training vibe out there to a fantastically wide audience and for generally putting up with us.